Keeping~up~your~ spirits Therapy

Keeping-up-your-spirits Therapy

written by
Linda Allison-Lewis

illustrated by
R.W. Alley

ONE
CARING
PLACE
Abbey Press

Text © 1991 Linda Allison-Lewis
Illustrations © 1991 St. Meinrad Archabbey
Published by One Caring Place
Abbey Press
St. Meinrad, Indiana 47577

Library of Congress Catalog Number
91-75415

ISBN 0-87029-242-0

Printed in the United States of America

Foreword

Whether we're struggling with illness, grief, or some other adversity, or just straining our survival skills for coping with a hectic lifestyle, we all need to boost our spirits from time to time. Often we overlook our own inner ability to handle difficulties and accept challenges in a way that lets us emerge stronger and happier with ourselves.

Keeping-up-your-spirits Therapy can show you how to awaken your true potential for self-help simply and in spite of your problems.

May these 35 insights, with R.W. Alley's delightful illustrations, help you to draw on your own strengths, sense God's constant presence, and experience peace, self-love, and healing during the toughest of times. May they invite you to find the blessings that often hide in unlikely places.

1.

Have a good attitude.
It's healthier than a plate
full of carrots.

2.

Cultivate your sense of humor. Laughter hides in strange places.

3.

Make a list of your talents.
You'll be amazed at yourself.

4.

Think of a special friend.
There's someone who loves
you because you're you.

5.

Keep things simple. You'll have more time for fun.

6.

Forgive someone you're angry at. You'll feel light as a feather.

7.

Forgive yourself in an instant.
God does!

8.

Make the best of what you have. You'll be amazed at its value.

9.

See problems as opportunities.
Don't dwell on them. Work
on finding solutions.

10.

Replace your fears with faith.
And then let go.

_11._

Don't despair. A broken heart can mend if you give God all the pieces.

12.

Don't run from the sad times. They can be opportunities to draw on strengths that have been sleeping.

13.

Cherish your memories. Recall those that make you smile.

14.

Live without making judgments. Acceptance brings joy.

15.

Abandon unnecessary guilt.
It's extra baggage you don't
need to carry.

16.

Pursue inner peace. It's the deepest of all blessings.

17.

Live in the moment. If you dwell on the past, you'll miss what's wonderful today.

18.

Live in the moment. If you focus on the future, you'll miss the freedom of today.

19.

Have faith in yourself.
Refuse to believe in the
word impossible.

20.

Let loose of what you can't control. Serenity will be yours.

21.

When you're having a bad day,
tell someone. A shared burden
is always lighter.

22.

Bask in the sunshine.
It'll warm your heart.

23.

Accept each part of yourself.
God did a remarkable job.

24.

Welcome new challenges. If God gives you a task, it will come with directions.

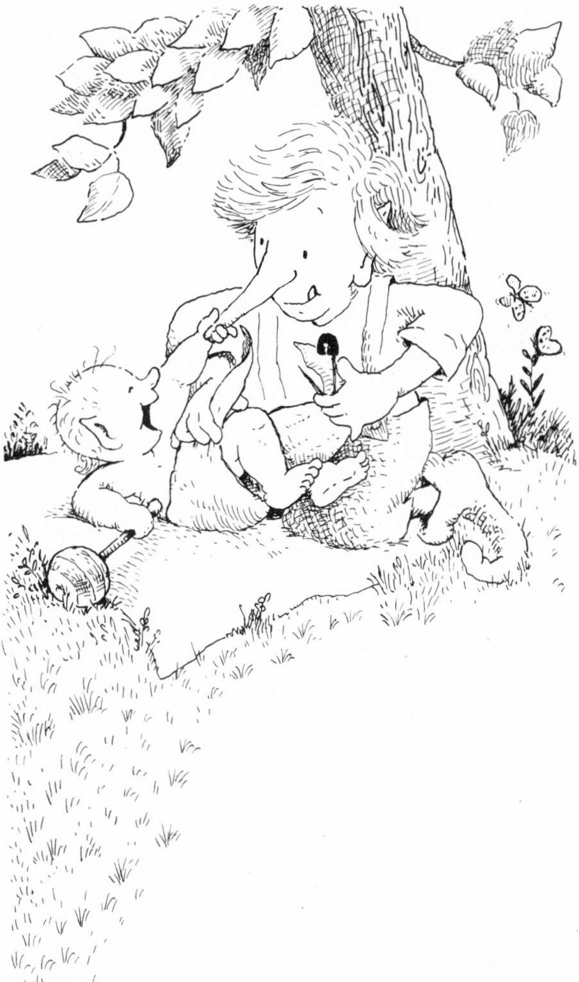

25.

Slow down. There's no telling what you might miss.

26.

Don't tear yourself down.
You have innate worth.

27.

Never compare yourself to another. You were formed with great precision.

28.

Accept others without conditions. It's the very essence of love.

29.

When everything is upside down, rest if you must—but don't quit.

30.

Accept suffering as a way
of uncovering true values.
You may not feel it,
but you're growing.

31.

Pray. God lifts the dark clouds when you pour out your troubles.

32.

Start your day with faith. God will give you the strength to do whatever is necessary.

33.

Set a small goal for yourself.
Accomplishments feel good.

34.

Offer someone love today.
You'll be pleased when it
returns to you.

35.

Know that each day of your life is a gift. Have you thanked your Creator today?

Linda Allison-Lewis is an author and a popular speaker on family issues and abstinence among teens. She is also the food columnist for *Kentucky Living* magazine. She has three children and writes from her home in Louisville, Kentucky.

Illustrator for the Abbey Press Elf-help Books, **R.W. Alley** also illustrates and writes children's books. He lives in Barrington, Rhode Island, with his wife, daughter, and son.

The Story of the Abbey Press Elves

The engaging figures that populate the Abbey Press "elf-help" line of publications and products first appeared in 1987 on the pages of a small self-help book called *Be-good-to-yourself Therapy*. Shaped by the publishing staff's vision and defined in R.W. Alley's inventive illustrations, they lived out author Cherry Hartman's gentle, self-nurturing advice with charm, poignancy, and humor.

Reader response was so enthusiastic that more Elf-help Books were soon under way, a still-growing series that has inspired a line of related gift products.

The especially endearing character featured in the early books—sporting a cap with a mood-changing candle in its peak—has since been joined by a spirited female elf with flowers in her hair.

These two exuberant, sensitive, resourceful, kindhearted, lovable sprites, along with their lively elfin community, reveal what's truly important as they offer messages of joy and wonder, playfulness and co-creation, wholeness and serenity, the miracle of life and the mystery of God's love.

With wisdom and whimsy, these little creatures with long noses demonstrate the elf-help way to a rich and fulfilling life.

Elf-help Books

...adding "a little character" and a lot
of help to self-help reading!

Trust-in-God Therapy
#20119 $4.95   ISBN 0-87029-322-2

Elf-help for Overcoming Depression
#20134 $4.95   ISBN 0-87029-315-X

New Baby Therapy
#20140 $4.95   ISBN 0-87029-307-9

Grief Therapy for Men
#20141 $4.95   ISBN 0-87029-306-0

Living From Your Soul
#20146 $4.95   ISBN 0-87029-303-6

Teacher Therapy
#20145 $4.95   ISBN 0-87029-302-8

Be-good-to-your-family Therapy
#20154 $4.95   ISBN 0-87029-300-1

Stress Therapy
#20153 $4.95   ISBN 0-87029-301-X

Making-sense-out-of-suffering Therapy
#20156 $4.95   ISBN 0-87029-296-X

Get Well Therapy
#20157 $4.95   ISBN 0-87029-297-8

Anger Therapy
#20127 $4.95   ISBN 0-87029-292-7

Caregiver Therapy
#20164 $4.95   ISBN 0-87029-285-4

Self-esteem Therapy
#20165 $4.95   ISBN 0-87029-280-3

Take-charge-of-your-life Therapy
#20168 $4.95   ISBN 0-87029-271-4

Work Therapy
#20166 $4.95   ISBN 0-87029-276-5

Everyday-courage Therapy
#20167 $4.95   ISBN 0-87029-274-9

Peace Therapy
#20176 $4.95   ISBN 0-87029-273-0

Friendship Therapy
#20174 $4.95   ISBN 0-87029-270-6

Christmas Therapy (color edition)
#20175 $5.95   ISBN 0-87029-268-4

Grief Therapy
#20178 $4.95   ISBN 0-87029-267-6

More Be-good-to-yourself Therapy
#20180 $3.95   ISBN 0-87029-262-5

Happy Birthday Therapy
#20181 $4.95   ISBN 0-87029-260-9

Forgiveness Therapy
#20184 $4.95   ISBN 0-87029-258-7

Keep-life-simple Therapy
#20185 $4.95   ISBN 0-87029-257-9

Be-good-to-your-body Therapy
#20188 $4.95   ISBN 0-87029-255-2

Celebrate-your-womanhood Therapy
#20189 $4.95   ISBN 0-87029-254-4

Acceptance Therapy (color edition)
#20182 $5.95   ISBN 0-87029-259-5

Acceptance Therapy
#20190 $4.95   ISBN 0-87029-245-5

Keeping-up-your-spirits Therapy
#20195 $4.95   ISBN 0-87029-242-0

Play Therapy
#20200 $4.95   ISBN 0-87029-233-1

Slow-down Therapy
#20203 $4.95   ISBN 0-87029-229-3

One-day-at-a-time Therapy
#20204 $4.95   ISBN 0-87029-228-5

Prayer Therapy
#20206 $4.95   ISBN 0-87029-225-0

Be-good-to-your-marriage Therapy
#20205 $4.95   ISBN 0-87029-224-2

Be-good-to-yourself Therapy (hardcover)
#20196 $10.95   ISBN 0-87029-243-9

Be-good-to-yourself Therapy
#20255 $4.95   ISBN 0-87029-209-9

Available at your favorite bookstore or directly from us at: One Caring Place, Abbey Press Publications, St. Meinrad, IN 47577. Or call 1-800-325-2511.